Flashrevise
Pocketbook

AS UK Government & Politics

Philip Allan Updates, an imprint of Hodder Education, an Hachette UK company, Market Place, Deddington, Oxfordshire OX15 0SE

Orders

Bookpoint Ltd, 130 Milton Park, Abingdon, Oxfordshire OX14 4SB

tel: 01235 827827   fax: 01235 400401   e-mail: education@bookpoint.co.uk

Lines are open 9.00 a.m.–5.00 p.m., Monday to Saturday, with a 24-hour message answering service. You can also order through our website: www.philipallan.co.uk

© Eric Magee and Paul Fairclough 2010
ISBN 978-1-4441-0783-8

213083

First published in 2005 as *Flashrevise Cards*

Impression number   5   4   3   2   1
Year   2014   2013   2012   2011   2010

Printed in Spain

Hachette UK's policy is to use papers that are natural, renewable and recyclable products and made from wood grown in sustainable forests. The logging and manufacturing processes are expected to conform to the environmental regulations of the country of origin.

P01808

Democracy

Q1 What is direct democracy?

Q2 What problems are associated with direct democracy?

Q3 Define representative democracy.

Q4 Distinguish between direct and representative democracy.

A1 A political system in which decisions are taken by people rather than by representatives acting on their behalf.

A2 Not possible with large numbers of voters; people do not want continuous participation; most people lack the knowledge and expertise to make informed decisions.

A3 A political system in which citizens elect representatives to make decisions of government on their behalf.

A4 The key distinction is between direct and indirect participation.

***examiner's* note** The UK is a representative democracy with representative institutions such as the House of Commons.

***evaluation* point** Direct democracy is not practical in a state with large numbers of people, but aspects of it can be found in the UK in the use of referendums, e.g. those on devolution in Scotland and Wales in 1997, on a regional assembly for the North East in 2004 and on the introduction of AV for Westminster elections in 2011.

 ANSWERS

Types of democracy

Q1 What is liberal democracy?

Q2 Is the UK a pluralist democracy? Explain your answer.

Q3 Is the UK a parliamentary democracy? Explain your answer.

Q4 Why are totalitarian regimes not seen to be 'real' democracies?

ANSWERS

A1 Limited government is the essence of liberal democracy. There is minimal government regulation but the state encourages participation and protects the rights of citizens.

A2 Yes. A pluralist system of government allows public participation, particularly through the activities of pressure groups that are free to express differing and conflicting points of view.

A3 Yes. The House of Commons is democratically elected and therefore governs by the will of the people.

A4 In totalitarian regimes, people are often represented by a single individual or an elite. Elections may be held, but candidates who oppose the leader or the elite are not permitted.

***examiner's* note** Most Western democracies are liberal democracies. A core feature of a 'real' democracy is competition between parties representing differing viewpoints.

***evaluation* point** Arguably, pluralism has not been achieved in the UK because there is not equality of access and influence between competing groups.

 ANSWERS

Referendums

Q1 What is a referendum?

Q2 Distinguish between a referendum and an initiative.

Q3 Outline three key arguments for the use of referendums.

Q4 Outline three key arguments against the use of referendums.

ANSWERS

A1 A vote on a single issue put before the electorate by the government, usually in the form of a question requiring a 'yes' or 'no' answer.

A2 The central distinction is that a referendum is government initiated, whereas an initiative is when the electorate demands the right to be asked a question on an issue.

A3 They provide mandates for major constitutional changes, are a form of direct democracy and encourage political participation.

A4 They are inconsistent with the doctrine of parliamentary sovereignty, they may result in voter apathy and low turnouts, and effective alternatives to test public opinion, e.g. opinion polls, already exist.

***examiner's* note** Initiatives or propositions are used in many US states. If a citizen can get the support of a specified proportion of the state's population, the question is put to the public vote.

***evaluation* point** A referendum may include more than one question. The Scottish referendum asked one question about devolution and another on whether the proposed Scottish Parliament should have tax-varying powers.

 ANSWERS

Use of referendums

Q1 Referendums are 'devices alien to our traditions'. True or false? Explain your answer.

Q2 List three issues on which referendums have been held.

Q3 Explain why these issues were put to a referendum.

Q4 Do referendums widen democratic participation? Explain your answer.

ANSWERS

- **A1** True. In a representative democracy, representatives are traditionally elected to govern on behalf of the electorate and they are not expected to ask about other issues between elections.
- **A2** Continued membership of the EEC (1975); devolution for Scotland and Wales (1997); the introduction of AV for Westminster elections (2011).
- **A3** The Labour Party was divided over Europe and this was seen as a way of uniting it. Devolution was a major constitutional change. A referendum on AV was part of the agreement to form the Conservative–Lib Dem coalition government after the 2010 general election.
- **A4** Yes. Voters get an additional opportunity to participate in the democratic process.

examiner's note There have been about 31 local referendums on US-style mayors. Will this coalition government use referendums in the way New Labour did to legitimise major changes?

evaluation point Referendums may be 'alien to our traditions', but they legitimise major constitutional changes and give them a degree of permanence (entrenchment).

 ANSWERS

Mayoral referendums

Q1 Why have there been referendums in the UK for US-style mayors?

Q2 Suggest reasons why there have been low turnouts in these referendums.

Q3 Should mayoral elections go ahead on the basis of a 'yes' vote on a low turnout?

Q4 Do low turnouts place a question mark over the legitimacy of the actions of these new mayors?

ANSWERS

A1 It is one of the ideas that the new Labour government of 1997 had for reinvigorating local democracy and countering voter apathy. The coalition government appears to favour increasing the number of elected city mayors.

A2 The electorate could feel apathy towards yet another election in addition to local, European and general elections. Turnout is traditionally low for local elections. The cost of installing and remunerating a mayor could raise council tax. It is unclear how mayors fit into the existing political structure.

A3 Yes. A democracy is more concerned with a majority verdict than with actual numbers of voters.

A4 In theory yes, but in practice they are unlikely to do so.

***examiner's* note** There had been 31 referendums for US-style mayors by 2005. Turnout was between 18% and 36% of the electorate. There may be more in the future.

***evaluation* point** The controversial Mayor of Middlesbrough was elected on a 34% turnout but such has been his success that he was re-elected in 2005 and 2009.

 ANSWERS

Future of referendums

Q1 Local referendums on issues such as council tax increases and congestion charges have been held. Why?

Q2 Will initiatives be introduced next? Explain your answer.

Q3 Should the UK allow recalls of elected officials?

Q4 Do you think the wider use of referendums would reinvigorate democracy?

ANSWERS

A1 Issues such as council tax increases and congestion charges are controversial and referendums show local councils what local people think about such proposals.

A2 Possibly. Referendums are top-down, i.e. initiated by central or local government. Initiatives are bottom-up, i.e. initiated by citizens, and citizens are increasingly making their voices heard on issues that concern them.

A3 Yes. Not currently used in the UK but will be used to allow voters to recall MPs in the light of the MPs' expenses scandal.

A4 They have the potential to do so, but low turnout suggests they are not doing so at present.

examiner's **note** In February 2005, on a turnout of 65%, Edinburgh voters rejected a congestion charging system with 75% voting no and 24% voting yes.

evaluation **point** If a government is serious about reinvigorating democracy, perhaps it should consider introducing initiatives. Other ideas, e.g. all-postal ballots and 'e-democracy', are being piloted in an attempt to reinvigorate democracy.

Is the UK democratic?

Q1 Present the case for the wider use of referendums.

Q2 Outline three ways in which the UK can be considered democratic.

Q3 Outline three ways in which the UK is not democratic.

Q4 Does the creation of a coalition government after the 2010 general election make the UK more or less democratic?

ANSWERS

A1 There will be important constitutional changes requiring consent, e.g. AV for Westminster elections. Future governments may be divided on an important issue, as Labour was in 1975.

A2 There are free and fair elections; parties and pressure groups operate freely; rule of law exists.

A3 There is an unfair electoral system, unelected House of Lords and no entrenched Bill of Rights.

A4 More democratic: the coalition represents 59% of those who voted. Less democratic: the voters did not vote for the compromise policies in the Coalition Agreement.

***examiner's* note** The defects in UK democracy exist because the UK constitution has evolved over time without revolutions, which often result in the introduction of new, more democratic constitutions.

***evaluation* point** The UK has all the features of a pluralist democracy, e.g. parties, trade unions and pressure groups that operate freely within the law. However, power is often transferred from elected bodies to unelected quangos.

 ANSWERS

What is a constitution?

Q1 What is a constitution?

Q2 Explain the term 'constitutional government'.

Q3 Political behaviour that is in accordance with accepted rules and norms is constitutional. True or false?

Q4 What is meant by 'unconstitutional'?

ANSWERS

A1 A legal framework detailing the composition and responsibilities of the institutions of government and describing their relationship both with each other and with the country's citizens.

A2 Government that functions according to rules laid down in a constitution. It therefore implies the operation of constraints on the exercise of power.

A3 True.

A4 Falling outside the accepted rules and norms of the political system.

***examiner's* note** Both the UK and USA have constitutional government, although they operate under different types of constitution. The UK has an uncodified constitution whereas the US has a codified one.

***evaluation* point** Attempts to change the constitutional status of Northern Ireland within the UK by violence are unconstitutional.

Codified and uncodified constitutions

Q1 What is a codified constitution?

Q2 What is an uncodified constitution?

Q3 Should the UK have a codified constitution?

ANSWERS ▶▶

A1 This is when the laws, rules and principles specifying how a state is to be governed are set out in a single, legally entrenched constitutional document.

A2 This is when the laws, rules and principles specifying how a state is to be governed are not set out in a single, legally entrenched document but are found in a variety of sources, such as statute law and EU law.

A3 Yes. Provides greater clarity on what is or is not constitutional. Citizens' rights better protected.

No. Would end flexibility of existing uncodified constitution. Difficult to amend. Too much power to judges.

***examiner's* note** Use the terms 'codified' and 'uncodified' rather than 'written' and 'unwritten'.

***evaluation* point** Whether a codified or uncodified constitution is better is the subject of debate involving questions of flexibility, reliability and certainty.

 **ANSWERS**

Sources of the constitution

Q1 Conventions and common law are sources of the UK constitution. True or false?

Q2 Name three other sources of the UK constitution.

Q3 Give two examples of conventions.

Q4 What are authoritative works?

ANSWERS

A1 True.

A2 Statute law; authoritative works; European Union law.

A3 The monarch having to assent to Acts of Parliament; the doctrine of collective ministerial responsibility.

A4 Legal and political texts that have become accepted as works of authority on the UK constitution, e.g. A. V. Dicey, *An Introduction to the Study of the Law of the Constitution*.

***examiner's* note** Common law includes customs and precedents that relate to the monarchy, such as the royal prerogative. This involves powers exercised in the name of the Crown, e.g. to declare war and negotiate treaties.

***evaluation* point** Prerogative powers no longer rest with the monarch. Government ministers exercise prerogative powers in the name of the Crown. It is the prime minister, for example, who declares war, decides the date of the general election and appoints government ministers.

Key principles of the UK constitution (1)

Q1 Membership of the European Union (EU) is a key characteristic of the constitution. True or false?

Q2 List four key principles of the constitution.

Q3 What is parliamentary sovereignty?

Q4 Define the rule of law.

ANSWERS ▶▶

A1 True.

A2 Parliamentary sovereignty; the rule of law; the unitary state; parliamentary government under a constitutional monarch.

A3 The central doctrine of the UK constitution which states that Parliament is the supreme law-making body in the country. Parliament cannot bind future parliaments in decision making. Its decisions cannot be overturned by any higher authority.

A4 A system of rule in which the relationship between the state and the individual is governed by law, protecting the individual from arbitrary state action.

***examiner's* note** Some argue that parliamentary sovereignty has been undermined by the UK's international obligations, e.g. membership of the EU and the supremacy of EU law over Acts of Parliament.

***evaluation* point** A. V. Dicey, writing in the nineteenth century, regarded the rule of law as one of the 'twin pillars of the constitution', the other being parliamentary sovereignty.

Key principles of the UK constitution (2)

Q1 What is a unitary state?

Q2 What is parliamentary government?

Q3 Define constitutional monarchy.

Q4 Outline one constitutional implication of UK membership of the EU.

ANSWERS

A1 A political system in which the central authority holds governmental power exclusively, with no autonomous powers residing in any other body.

A2 A political system in which government takes place through parliament, blurring the boundaries between the executive and legislative branches.

A3 A political system in which the monarch is the formal head of state, but the monarch's legal powers are exercised by government ministers.

A4 The UK courts apply EU law directly, and where questions of interpretation of EU law arise, they are referred to the European Court of Justice.

***examiner's* note** Do not confuse the European Court of Justice with the European Court of Human Rights.

***evaluation* point** Although there are levels of government other than the national government in London, the Westminster Parliament can restrict their powers and even abolish them.

(12) ANSWERS

UK constitutional principles in flux?

Q1 Identify a way in which UK membership of the EU can be said to have undermined parliamentary sovereignty.

Q2 Has the programme of devolution since 1997 undermined the unitary state?

Q3 To what extent can anti-terrorist legislation be seen as limiting the rule of law?

ANSWERS

A1 The European Communities Act (1972) gave European Community (later European Union) law precedence over UK statute law when the two conflicted.

A2 No. The UK may appear to be moving towards a more federal arrangement, but power has simply been devolved rather than transferred. All recent changes can be reversed by Act of Parliament, in theory at least. Some refer to this as quasi-federalism.

A3 Treatment of terrorist suspects under such legislation undermines some elements of the rule of law identified by Dicey. Those imprisoned in the UK under the Anti-terrorism, Crime and Security Act (2001) were effectively being punished without trial.

***examiner's* note** The extension of qualified majority voting has limited the UK's ability to block EU measures.

***evaluation* point** The notion of parliamentary sovereignty has always been limited in practice by political realities, including international demands.

 **ANSWERS**

Strengths and weaknesses of the UK constitution

Q1 Outline two strengths of the UK constitution.

Q2 How is government accountable?

Q3 Outline two weaknesses of the UK constitution.

Q4 Which pre-democratic elements survive?

ANSWERS

A1 The rule of law protects the rights of citizens. The government is responsible — it is accountable to Parliament and the electorate.

A2 It is answerable in Parliament for its actions and an unpopular government is likely to lose the next general election.

A3 Constitutional rules and conventions are unclear and can be overridden because the UK constitution is uncodified. Pre-democratic elements survive.

A4 An unelected House of Lords and a hereditary monarchy.

examiner's **note** The convention of ministerial responsibility is unclear, with very few ministers resigning even when serious errors appear to have been made.

evaluation **point** Power in the UK is concentrated at the centre and a government with a strong majority can force most things through Parliament, e.g. the decision to go to war in Iraq.

Blair and constitutional reform, 1997–2001 (1)

Q1 What constitutional reforms did Labour introduce between 1997 and 2001?

Q2 Outline the reforms concerned with rights.

Q3 What happened in relation to devolution and decentralisation?

Q4 Outline the changes in Northern Ireland.

ANSWERS

A1 There were reforms in all the areas outlined in the manifesto: devolution and decentralisation; rights and elections; parties and referendums.

A2 The Human Rights Act (1998) enshrined most of the provisions of the European Convention on Human Rights in UK law. A Freedom of Information Act was passed.

A3 Scottish Parliament and Welsh Assembly established; a mayor elected and strategic authority set up (the Greater London Authority) in London; Regional Development Agencies set up in London.

A4 The Northern Ireland Act (1998) established a Northern Ireland Assembly and power-sharing executive.

examiner's note The Freedom of Information Act did not come into force until 2005 and disappointed liberal reformers because of its limited nature.

evaluation point The Human Rights Act meant that citizens could seek redress in UK courts without having to go to the European Court of Human Rights in Strasbourg.

Blair and constitutional reform, 1997–2001 (2)

Q1 What reforms to do with referendums were introduced between 1997 and 2001?

Q2 Outline the intention of the Political Parties, Elections and Referendum Act, 2000 (PPER).

Q3 What was set up to deal with electoral reform?

Q4 Evaluate Labour's constitutional reforms of 1997–2001.

ANSWERS

A1 The Referendums Act (1997) provided for devolution referendums in Scotland and Wales. There was also a referendum in London for an elected mayor and assembly.

A2 To regulate the conduct of elections and referendums.

A3 An independent commission was set up under Lord Jenkins and reported in 1998, recommending the adoption of a mixed electoral system called AV plus.

A4 They were arguably the most important package of constitutional reforms introduced in the modern UK.

***examiner's* note** The PPER Act set an upper limit on national campaign expenditure by political parties at general elections and established an independent Electoral Commission to monitor elections and referendums.

***evaluation* point** Although Labour's constitutional reform package was significant, the reforms were not revolutionary — there was no UK bill of rights or a codified constitution introduced.

Blair and constitutional reform, 2001–2007

Q1 What did Labour pledge in its 2001 general election manifesto?

Q2 Outline the constitutional reforms introduced by Labour between 2001 and 2007.

Q3 How have Labour's constitutional reforms been criticised?

Q4 What would constitute an alternative reform package?

ANSWERS

A1 Complete Lords reform; modernisation of the Commons; to create directly elected regional government in England; a referendum on the euro; to review the new electoral systems.

A2 Further modernisation of the Commons; proposals for further reform of the Lords; new Department of Constitutional Affairs set up; the creation of a UK Supreme Court; regional referendums on regional assemblies.

A3 From the right-wing: too extensive and damaging to the constitution; from a liberal perspective: too limited and lacking coherence.

A4 Codified constitution; UK bill of rights; elected upper chamber; proportional representation for general elections; state funding of political parties; reform (or abolition) of the monarchy.

examiner's **note** Reform of the House of Lords was left unfinished.

evaluation **point** Labour's reforms between 2001 and 2007 have been criticised as ill-thought-out.

(17) ANSWERS

Brown and constitutional reform, 2007–2010

Q1 What did Brown propose in 'The Governance of Britain' Green Paper?

Q2 What did Brown achieve as a constitutional reformer?

Q3 Did Labour's reforms (1997–2010) result in a new constitutional settlement?

ANSWERS

A1 Four key objectives: limiting powers of the executive, making the executive more accountable, reinvigorating democracy and improving the relationship between the citizen and the state.

A2 Very little. Blown off course by economic crisis and MPs' expenses scandal. After expenses scandal reform revisited but then came the 2010 general election.

A3 Yes. Most extensive series of reforms in modern times.

No. Unfinished and no overarching vision.

***examiner's* note** Although Brown saw himself as a constitutional reformer it was Blair who introduced the significant reforms.

***evaluation* point** More radical reforms, such as a codified constitution and electoral reform for Westminster, were not attempted.

The 2010 coalition and constitutional reform (1)

Q1 What constitutional reforms did Labour propose in its 2010 manifesto?

Q2 What constitutional reforms did the Conservatives propose in their 2010 manifesto?

Q3 What constitutional reforms did the Lib Dems include in their 2010 manifesto?

A1 Referendum on elected second chamber; fixed-term parliaments; recall of MPs; referendum on alternative vote; all-party commission on a written constitution.

A2 Mainly elected Lords; recall of MPs; cut number of MPs; equalise constituency sizes; directly elected police chiefs.

A3 Fully elected Lords; referendum on STV for general elections; cut number of MPs by 150; codified constitution subject to approval in a referendum.

***examiner's* note** All three parties committed to significant constitutional change.

***evaluation* point** The differences between the three parties were on the extent of the reforms proposed, e.g. a mainly elected versus a fully elected Lords.

The 2010 coalition and constitutional reform (2)

Q1 What did the Coalition Agreement say about constitutional reform?

Q2 What did the coalition partners gain and lose in the Coalition Agreement?

Q3 Which reforms will be implemented first?

ANSWERS

A1 Referendum on introduction of AV; reduction in number of constituencies; more equal-sized constituencies; 5-year fixed-term parliaments; recall of MPs; wholly or mainly elected Lords; Commons reforms.

A2 Both had to compromise on key issues, e.g. electoral reform for Westminster, but it appears as a genuine compromise between their policy positions.

A3 Referendum on AV; fixed-term parliaments; arrangements for dissolution within the fixed term; more equally sized constituencies; reduction in number of MPs.

examiner's **note** There may be opposition not just from Labour but within the coalition parties to some of these reforms.

evaluation **point** These reforms could be even more significant than New Labour's constitutional reforms.

Elections

Q1 Define the term 'representation'.

Q2 Outline the functions of elections.

Q3 What are by-elections?

Q4 Discuss the significance of by-elections.

ANSWERS

A1 In a representative democracy elections allow the electorate (a large group) to elected reperesentatives (a smaller group) to act on their behalf.

A2 Participation; representation; legitimacy; accountability; choosing a government.

A3 Elections held between general elections.

A4 They are often used by voters to give their verdict on how the government is doing. They can almost amount to a referendum on the performance of the government.

***examiner's* note** By-elections are usually held due to a vacancy arising as the result of the death or resignation of the sitting MP.

***evaluation* point** A disputed 1997 general election outcome in Winchester resulted in a High Court decision that a by-election should be held because a number of ballot papers crucial to the result had not been counted.

Coalition government

Q1 Define coalition government.

Q2 What is majority government?

Q3 Explain the term 'minority government'.

Q4 What is a coalition agreement?

ANSWERS

A1 A government composed of members from more than one political party.

A2 A government composed of members from one political party, resulting from that party winning more seats in the House of Commons at a general election than all the other parties added together.

A3 A government formed by a political party without an overall majority of MPs in the House of Commons.

A4 An agreement on policy and other issues negotiated after an election by the partners in a coalition to form the basis of coalition government.

***examiner's* note** Minority governments are rare at Westminster, but from 1976 to 1979 there was a minority Labour government.

***evaluation* point** The coalition government formed after the 2010 general election is the first to be formed in over 50 years so it is a new feature of contemporary Westminster politics.

UK electoral systems

Q1 Which electoral system is used for general elections to the Westminster Parliament?

Q2 Which systems are used for other UK elections?

Q3 Outline the key features of the supplementary vote.

Q4 What kind of system is the additional member system?

ANSWERS >>

A1 First-past-the-post (FPTP).

A2 Additional member system for Scottish Parliament, Welsh Assembly and Greater London Assembly; supplementary vote used for directly elected mayors; single transferable vote in Northern Ireland; regional list system for European Parliament.

A3 In single-member constituencies, voters make first and second preferences; a candidate with more than 50% first preferences wins, or the two candidates with most first-preference votes are allocated the second-preference votes of eliminated candidates until one is elected.

A4 A hybrid system. Some candidates are elected by a simple plurality in single-member constituencies and others through regional party lists to ensure a degree of proportionality.

examiner's **note** The referendum on AV for Westminster elections in 2011 could be the end of FPTP.

evaluation **point** AV is not a proportional system and can produce less proportional outcomes than FPTP.

(23) ANSWERS

First-past-the-post (FPTP)

Q1 How does the FPTP system work?

Q2 Present criticisms of the FPTP system.

Q3 Present arguments in support of the FPTP system.

Q4 Why is there pressure for electoral reform?

ANSWERS

A1 The candidate with the most votes wins even if the combined votes of the other candidates are more.

A2 It disadvantages small parties; results in wasted votes; limits voter choice; results in adversarial politics.

A3 It is easy to understand; part of our traditions; cheap to operate; retains the link between constituents and MPs; normally results in strong, majority government; excludes extremist parties from parliamentary representation.

A4 Proportional representation has been introduced for many other UK elections, so why not for general elections? Is it acceptable in a democracy to win 23% of the vote and 8.8% of the seats (Lib Dems in 2010)?

***examiner's* note** FPTP is a simple plurality system in single-member constituencies.

***evaluation* point** FPTP does not always produce a clear winner. It did not do so in 1964, 1974 (February), 1974 (October) and 2010.

Alternative vote and supplementary vote

Q1 How does the alternative vote (AV) system work?

Q2 In what way does the supplementary vote (SV) system differ from AV?

Q3 Are these two systems proportional or majoritarian?

Q4 Why did the Electoral Reform Society (ERS) think that AV would be better than SV as a system for electing the mayor of London?

ANSWERS

A1 Voters rank candidates in order of preference (1, 2, 3, etc). If no candidate receives more than half of the votes, the bottom candidate is eliminated and their votes transferred. This continues until a candidate secures more than 50% of the votes cast.

A2 Under SV, the failure of any candidate to secure over half of the vote results in all but the top two candidates being eliminated and their votes being transferred.

A3 Majoritarian.

A4 The ERS was concerned that in a four-horse race for mayor under SV, voters would have to guess which two candidates would be left in the final run-off before casting their votes.

***examiner's* note** In 2010 the Conservative–Lib Dem coalition promised a referendum on the introduction of the AV system for use in elections to the Westminster Parliament.

***evaluation* point** AV might lead to a more proportional result for parties such as the Liberal Democrats. As many voters' second preference, they could win seats where no candidate has secured sufficient first preferences.

 ANSWERS

London mayoral and assembly elections

Q1 Which type of electoral system is used for mayor of London and other mayoral elections?

Q2 Which electoral system is used for the London Assembly?

Q3 Why must parties reach a 5% threshold before they are entitled to representation in the London Assembly?

Q4 What has been the impact on party representation in the London Assembly?

ANSWERS

A1 Supplementary vote. Voters make a first- and second-preference choice among candidates. A candidate getting over 50% of first-preference votes is elected. Otherwise, all but the top two candidates are eliminated and their votes transferred. The candidate with most first- and second-preference votes combined is elected.

A2 Additional member system (AMS). Fourteen of the 25 members are elected by FPTP and the remaining 11 'additional' members from a list in proportion to each party's share of the vote in the FPTP election.

A3 To make it more difficult for extremist parties such as the British National Party to win seats.

A4 It has produced multi-party representation.

***examiner's* note** The use of SV in the first London mayoral election led to the elimination of the Labour candidate, Frank Dobson.

***evaluation* point** The Electoral Reform Society preferred alternative vote (AV) for the London mayoral election and single transferable vote (STV) for the assembly.

Single transferable vote

Q1 What is proportional representation (PR)?

Q2 Outline the key features of the single transferable vote (STV) form of PR.

Q3 Outline strengths of STV.

Q4 Outline weaknesses of STV.

ANSWERS

A1 An electoral system where seats in the legislature are allocated in broad proportion to the distribution of votes.

A2 Takes place in multi-member constituencies; voters rank candidates in order of preference; candidates are elected by reaching a quota.

A3 It is a proportional system; votes are not wasted; voters have more choice; small parties can get candidates elected; independents have a better chance of being elected.

A4 It is a complicated system of counting and transferring votes; it leads to coalition governments, which some see as a form of weak government; it weakens the MP–constituency link present under FPTP.

***examiner's* note** STV is used in Northern Ireland for elections to the Northern Ireland Assembly, local authorities and the European Parliament, and for local elections in Scotland.

***evaluation* point** STV gives voters a great deal of choice because second and subsequent preferences count and voters can express a preference between candidates from the same party.

(27) ANSWERS

Northern Ireland elections

Q1 Why is proportional representation (PR) used for elections to the Northern Ireland Assembly?

Q2 Why was the single transferable vote system of PR chosen?

Q3 What type of coalition was formed?

Q4 Why was this type of coalition formed?

ANSWERS

A1 Northern Ireland is a divided society with a majority of Protestants and a minority of Roman Catholics. Under FPTP it was a dominant-party state ruled by the Unionist Party (the Protestant party).

A2 To allow the various viewpoints in Northern Ireland to be represented in the assembly.

A3 A coalition representing all the main parties — the two main varieties of unionism and the two main varieties of nationalism/republicanism.

A4 To attempt to overcome traditional hostilities between Protestants and Catholics and between unionists and nationalists, by making them work together.

***examiner's* note** Tensions between the various parties resulted in the suspension of the Northern Ireland Assembly in October 2002 and the restoration of direct rule from Westminster.

***evaluation* point** Although there have been tensions and difficulties, the Northern Ireland Assembly and the power-sharing executive have survived.

Party lists

Q1 Explain the party list system.

Q2 Outline four advantages of the party list system.

Q3 Outline three disadvantages of the party list system.

Q4 What is a closed regional list system?

ANSWERS

A1 It is an electoral system in which voters choose from a list of candidates in large, multi-member constituencies, and seats are allocated according to the proportion of votes won by each political party. In open list systems, voters select from a list of individual candidates representing political parties and independent candidates. In closed list systems, voters can only select a party slate or independent candidate.

A2 It is a proportional system; votes are not wasted; it is fair to parties; small parties can win seats.

A3 It is unlikely to produce a clear winner; it results in coalition governments; there is no constituency representation.

A4 The voter is required to vote for a political party rather than a candidate.

examiner's note The closed regional list system is used for elections to the European Parliament.

evaluation point Closed list systems are criticised for giving too much power to the party leadership, who decide where a candidate is on the list and therefore who is likely to be elected.

(29) ANSWERS

European elections

Q1 Which type of proportional representation is used in elections for the European Parliament?

Q2 Why has this system been criticised?

Q3 Outline two advantages of list systems.

Q4 What impact has this system of proportional representation had on party representation?

ANSWERS

A1 The closed regional list system, where the order in which candidates are placed on the list is decided by the party leadership.

A2 Party leaders, not the voters, choose the order. In open list systems, voters can show a preference between candidates from the same party.

A3 They are clearly proportional and therefore fair to all parties. Open list systems give voters a wider choice.

A4 It has produced fragmented results with no clear winner.

examiner's note Small parties such as UKIP and the Green Party are able to gain representation under this system — 12 and 2 seats respectively in 2004.

evaluation point The SNP and Plaid Cymru, with concentrated support in Scotland and Wales respectively, do not benefit significantly from proportional representation, so PR does not always favour small parties.

Additional member system

Q1 Is the additional member system (AMS) a majoritarian or a proportional system?

Q2 In which UK elections is AMS used?

Q3 Outline at least one advantage and one disadvantage of this system.

ANSWERS

A1 Neither. It is a hybrid electoral system incorporating both majoritarian and proportional elements.

A2 First-past-the-post top-up (FPTP–TU), a variant of AMS, is used in elections to the Scottish Parliament, the Welsh Assembly and the Greater London Assembly.

A3 By offering a proportional, list-based top-up, FPTP–TU can be fairer on those parties that do not have enough support in a single FPTP constituency to win the contest. It does, however, create a two-class system of representatives — some with constituencies and some without.

***examiner's* note** The Conservatives secured 16.7% of the vote in Scotland in the 2010 general election, yet only won a single Scottish seat in the Westminster Parliament. In the 2007 Scottish Parliament election they secured just 4 FPTP seats but were awarded a further 13 top-up seats.

***evaluation* point** The introduction of AMS in Scotland resulted in a coalition government (Labour/LibDem) that brought significant changes in policy.

Devolution electoral systems

Q1 Which electoral system is used for elections to the Welsh Assembly and the Scottish Parliament?

Q2 What impact did this electoral system have on party representation in Scotland?

Q3 What impact did it have on party representation in Wales?

ANSWERS

A1 Additional member system (AMS); FPTP top-up (a hybrid system).

A2 Labour–Lib Dem coalitions after the 1999 and 2003 elections. A minority SNP government after 2007.

A3 A mixture of minority and coalition governments, including currently (2010) a Labour–Plaid Cymru coalition.

examiner's note The Conservatives failed to win a seat in either Scotland or Wales in the 1997 general election under FPTP, but won seats in the devolved institutions under a hybrid system.

evaluation point Although the Liberal Democrats came fourth in Scotland in 1999 and 2003, they entered government in coalition with Labour, the largest party.

Systems evaluated

Q1 How have the new electoral systems introduced in some UK elections since 1997 affected the political system?

Q2 What are coalition governments?

Q3 Does proportional representation produce weak governments? Explain your answer.

ANSWERS))

A1 They have resulted in: coalition and/or minority governments in the Scottish Parliament and Welsh Assembly; controversy over use of the closed regional list system for European elections; renewed demands for proportional representation in Westminster elections.

A2 Governments composed of members of more than one political party.

A3 Not necessarily. Although Italy's coalition governments have not always been stable, Germany's have normally been successful.

examiner's note Coalition governments at Westminster have been rare, but history was made after the 2010 general election when a Conservative–Liberal Democrat coalition government was formed.

evaluation point Opponents of electoral reform have used the coalition and minority governments in the Scottish Parliament and Welsh Assembly to warn that coalition and minority governments at Westminster would result if FPTP were abandoned, but in 2010 a coalition government resulted under FPTP.

 ANSWERS

Compulsory voting

Q1 What is compulsory voting?

Q2 Present arguments in favour of compulsory voting.

Q3 Present arguments against compulsory voting.

Q4 Are you in favour of or against compulsory voting? Give reasons for your answer.

ANSWERS

A1 A legal requirement of citizens to vote, as in Australia.

A2 It deals with the problem of low turnout, helps reduce the role of money in elections and enhances political literacy.

A3 It results in the 'tyranny of the majority', it is difficult to implement and it favours established and dominant parties. It compromises the right to vote.

A4 Either side may be taken. The key is to state clearly why you favour the side you have chosen.

***examiner's* note** Compulsory voting works as a corrective to low voter turnout. When it was abolished in the Netherlands in 1970, turnout fell by 10%.

***evaluation* point** The costs of compulsory voting, in terms of infringing individual freedoms and debasing political institutions through 'participation by force', may be too high.

A UK participation crisis?

Q1 Is there a participation crisis in the UK?

Q2 Does political participation matter?

Q3 How should falling levels of participation be tackled?

ANSWERS

A1 Yes. Low turnout at general elections. Disengagement from politics linked to lack of confidence in democratic institutions and a feeling there were no real differences between the parties.

A2 Yes. Low levels of participation undermine the legitimacy of political institutions and processes. Some evidence that the higher the levels of participation in a country the more effective its government is.

A3 Improve low voter turnout by measures such as encouraging more postal voting, use of e-democracy, compulsory voting and lowering the voting age.

***examiner's* note** Political participation may also be improved by renewing the UK's democratic institutions to involve citizens more directly in politics, e.g. wider use of referendums and citizens' juries.

***evaluation* point** Question the likely success of measures such as e-democracy, compulsory voting and lowering the voting age in improving political participation.

Political culture

Q1 What is meant by the term 'political culture'?

Q2 What elements were traditionally said to characterise UK political culture?

Q3 To what extent do these principles still hold true?

ANSWERS ▶▶

A1 Political culture is embodied in the opinions, attitudes and beliefs that define the citizenry's political behaviour.

A2 Homogeneity; consensus; deference.

A3 Homogeneity has arguably been undermined by the rise of mass immigration since the 1950s. The UK is now more commonly characterised as a multicultural society than a homogeneous one. The postwar consensus came under threat in the 1970s and gave way to a more confrontational, adversarial style of politics under Margaret Thatcher. Some feel that the rise of the mass media has led to the emergence of a less deferential society.

examiner's note Criticism of the monarchy in the popular press has been offered by some commentators as a sign of declining deference.

evaluation point Studies of political culture are always likely to be flawed, as they rely upon generalisations regarding the way in which individuals act. In reality, therefore, terms such as homogeneity, consensus and deference are always limited in their application.

Voting behaviour

Q1 How important is class in determining voting behaviour?

Q2 What is issue voting?

Q3 How important are regional factors in explaining voting behaviour?

Q4 Outline the role of the media in influencing how people vote.

ANSWERS

A1 Class was once seen as the main factor determining voting behaviour, but with class dealignment other factors became more important.

A2 A theory that voting is based on assessment of which party is most likely to deliver on key issues.

A3 Traditionally, there has been a north–south divide, with Labour stronger in the north and Conservatives stronger in the south. Since the 1970s, voting has varied more from region to region. Conservatives do less well in urban areas, Labour less well in rural areas.

A4 In 1997, Tony Blair thanked the *Sun* for 'its magnificent support'. The way party leaders court editors and proprietors shows that newspaper support is important.

examiner's note Issues are important, but in the 1992 general election Labour got the issues right and still lost.

evaluation point Anthony Heath and colleagues claim there is 'trendless fluctuation' in the working-class vote for Labour and that class alignment is still important.

 ANSWERS

Aligned and dealigned voting

Q1 What is aligned voting?

Q2 Outline reasons for aligned voting.

Q3 What is dealigned voting?

Q4 Outline reasons for dealigned voting.

ANSWERS

A1 A long-term and consistent inclination on the part of the electorate to vote for a particular party (party identification).

A2 Class-based voting; stable class system; strong partisan attachment to a particular party on the part of the electorate.

A3 The breakdown of the long-term and consistent inclination on the part of the electorate to vote for a particular party.

A4 Changing social structure; decline in class voting; decreased deference; decline in partisanship; increased influence of television and the media in general; perceived failure of parties in government.

***examiner's* note** Class and partisan alignment were significant features of voting behaviour from 1945 to the 1970s, after which dealignment was observed.

***evaluation* point** Aligned voting happened in a period of two-party dominance, when the two-party share of the vote was high. Electoral volatility, a fall in the two-party share of the vote and greater unpredictability are features of dealignment.

Tactical and protest voting

Q1 What is tactical voting?

Q2 What is protest voting?

Q3 Why does protest voting most often take place in contests between general elections?

A1 An individual votes for a candidate other than their first choice in order to prevent a third, even less 'desirable' candidate from being elected.

A2 An individual casts a vote against his/her usual party of choice to send a message to that party, often regarding a particular policy or the party's conduct in government.

A3 Most people engaging in protest voting do not want to see their party lose a general election; they want to register their disquiet over the direction of party policy. Protest voting between general elections is relatively low-risk.

***examiner's* note** Some commentators argued that tactical voting at the 2010 general election served to deny the Conservative Party a commons majority.

***evaluation* point** Tactical voting may be one consequence of the limited options open to voters under FPTP.

Issue-based voting

Q1 Why have issues become a more important determinant of voting behaviour in recent years?

Q2 Give two or more examples of issues playing a key role in recent elections.

Q3 Give an example of an election in which issues, though prominent, did not have a major influence on voting behaviour.

ANSWERS

A1 Due to the lessened importance of longer-term factors such as class and party identification.

A2 The 'Winter of Discontent' in 1979 was significant. The 'Falklands Factor' was said to have been an influence in 1983. The 1997 general election was played out against a backdrop of 'sleaze'.

A3 In the 2001 general election, the Labour government's handling of the fuel crisis and the foot-and-mouth crisis in 2000–01 did not appear to have a major effect on the outcome.

examiner's **note** Fears that the EU Constitution would become a big issue in a projected 2005 general election were said to have prompted Tony Blair to promise a referendum.

evaluation **point** The rise of issue voting is said to have made voting behaviour more volatile. This is because such issues are, by their very nature, less predictable than longer-term influences such as social class.

The media and voting behaviour

Q1 What do we mean by the term 'mass media'?

Q2 Define the term 'manipulative theory'.

Q3 Give one or more examples of the media being said to have significantly influenced the outcome of an election.

ANSWERS

A1 The mass media can be divided broadly into broadcast media (television, radio), the press (newspapers, journals, magazines) and 'new media' (internet).

A2 The belief that the media are controlled by an elite, who use them to preserve their own position and promote their own interests.

A3 The *Sun*'s support of the Conservatives in 1992 ('It's the *Sun* wot won it') and their decision to back Labour in 1997 ('It's the *Sun* wot swung it').

***examiner's* note** In 2004, Rupert Murdoch indicated that Labour could not be sure of the support of his newspapers at the next general election. In 2009 the *Sun* publicly backed David Cameron's Conservative Party.

***evaluation* point** Some argue that media influence is overstated. In the 1950s the US psychologist Festinger, for example, argued that people filter media content through three processes: selective exposure, selective perception and selective retention. They expose themselves to media that reflect their view, perceive only those which fit in with their view and only retain the information that supports their view.

 ANSWERS

Electoral campaigns and voting

Q1 Explain the purpose of election campaigns.

Q2 How important are general election campaigns?

Q3 What is a manifesto?

Q4 Victory gives a party a mandate for its policies. True or false? Explain your answer.

ANSWERS

A1 Election campaigns are a strategic effort by political parties and candidates to maximise their votes in an election.

A2 Evidence unclear. Most voters have made up their minds before the campaign begins but effective campaigns in marginal seats can change the outcome of the contest.

A3 A pre-election document produced by each political party outlining its proposals and pledges for government if it were to win.

A4 True. Policies are presented in the party's manifesto and victory is seen as an electoral mandate to implement those policies. For example, the Labour government increased the minimum wage after the 2001 general election because such an increase was promised in its manifesto and the voters had approved the policy.

examiner's note The drafting of a manifesto can be contentious because the party leadership is reluctant to take instructions as to its contents.

evaluation point The outcome of the 2010 general election has raised questions about the mandate. Nobody voted for the Coalition Agreement, which only emerged as a result of negotiations after the general election.

Composition of Parliament

Q1 What do we mean by the term 'parliament'?

Q2 Briefly outline the composition of the UK Parliament.

Q3 What do we mean by 'resemblance theory'?

Q4 Apply resemblance theory to the House of Commons.

ANSWERS

A1 It is an institution of government, comprising representatives elected by voters, whose functions are to debate, scrutinise and pass legislation.

A2 In July 2010, the House of Commons comprised 650 MPs and the Lords comprised 755 peers: 614 life peers, 92 hereditary peers, 26 bishops and 23 originally appointed as law lords.

A3 Legislators should be typical of the communities they serve, in order to reflect their communities' collective values and beliefs.

A4 The Commons does not reflect the UK population. After the 2010 general election, there were only 142 women and 26 ethnic minority MPs; over 25% of MPs in December 2010 had attended Oxford or Cambridge University.

***examiner's* note** At the 2005 general election, the number of MPs at Westminster was reduced from 659 to 646, because the number of Scottish constituencies was reduced from 72 to 59. Ahead of the 2010 general election the number of constituencies was increased from 646 to 650. This means that the number of seats required for a party to form a majority government is 326.

***evaluation* point** The influx of mostly Labour women MPs in 1997 was seen as a result of the party's use of all-women short-lists in some areas.

 43 ANSWERS

Functions of Parliament

Q1 What is a parliamentary system of government?

Q2 What is a presidential system of government?

Q3 List four key functions of Parliament.

Q4 How important is Parliament?

ANSWERS

A1 A political system in which the executive and the legislature are interconnected and the government is normally the majority party in the legislature.

A2 A political system in which the legislature and executive are distinct because of the separation of powers with separate elections for the executive and legislative branches. A president is at its head.

A3 Passing legislation; scrutiny of the executive; representation; recruitment of ministers.

A4 Some argue that power has passed from the legislature to the executive and that Parliament has become just a talking shop. Others argue that Parliament still has a role in shaping legislation.

***examiner's* note** The UK has a parliamentary system whereas the USA has a presidential system.

***evaluation* point** The UK executive still regards parliamentary approval as important, especially for major decisions. For example, approval was sought for the Iraq war, even though it was not legally required.

The legislative process (1)

Q1 What is a private bill?

Q2 What is a public bill?

Q3 How are Private Members' Bills introduced?

Q4 Why do Private Members' Bills normally fail?

ANSWERS ▶▶

A1 Proposed legislation, now relatively rare, intended to apply only to a particular company, public body or section of the population.

A2 Proposed legislation applying to the public as a whole. Most public bills are sponsored by the government. A second type of public bill is a Private Member's Bill.

A3 Two ways are 'ballot bills' and under the Ten Minute Rule.

A4 Due to lack of parliamentary time and the difficulty of ensuring voting support.

examiner's note Less than a quarter of Private Members' Bills introduced between 1990 and 1997 became law.

evaluation point In 1997 Michael Foster MP introduced a bill to ban hunting with dogs, which passed its second reading but ran out of time and therefore failed. The bill finally became law in 2005.

(45) ANSWERS

The legislative process (2)

Q1 What is a Green Paper?

Q2 What is a White Paper?

Q3 Outline the legislative process in parliament.

Q4 What is the role of the whips in the legislative process?

A1 A document in which the government outlines policies and proposed legislation, inviting comments and discussion. It is an early consultative stage in the legislative process.

A2 A document in which the government states its policy and announces intended legislation on a particular issue.

A3 Queen's speech; first reading; second reading; committee stage; report stage; third reading; House of Lords; royal assent.

A4 Government whips seek to ensure that government legislation gets through parliament with the necessary majorities.

***examiner's* note** A White Paper is the post-consultative stage in the legislative process and may be the subject of a debate in the House of Commons.

***evaluation* point** Although whips are generally successful, there are backbench revolts. In January 2004, 72 Labour MPs voted against the government over student 'top-up' fees.

Commons committees

Q1 What is a standing committee?

Q2 How is membership of standing committees decided?

Q3 What is a select committee?

Q4 What is the Select Committee on Standards and Privileges?

ANSWERS

A1 An ad hoc parliamentary committee consisting of 18–25 members whose function is to scrutinise the details of proposed legislation.

A2 Members are from different parties roughly in proportion to the make-up of the parties in the Commons.

A3 A permanent parliamentary committee with the function of investigating and scrutinising both the executive and aspects of the workings of the legislature.

A4 A relatively new non-departmental select committee established in the wake of the 'cash for questions' scandal to oversee the conduct and interests of MPs.

***examiner's* note** Non-departmental select committees can be permanent, e.g. Public Accounts Committee, or ad hoc, e.g. Committee on Standards in Public Life.

***evaluation* point** Demands for reform of departmental select committees to make them more effective have been only partially successful. For example, extra resources have been allocated, but attempts to reduce the influence of whips on the selection of committee members were rejected.

 ANSWERS

Parliamentary questions

Q1 What is Question Time?

Q2 Give reasons why questions are asked.

Q3 How important is Question Time?

Q4 Why has Question Time been criticised?

ANSWERS

A1 It is the opportunity for MPs to ask government ministers oral questions in the House of Commons or House of Lords. Prime Minister's Questions take place each Wednesday at noon for half an hour.

A2 To embarrass the government; to gain information; to raise a grievance on the part of a constituent.

A3 It is part of the process of scrutinising and holding the government to account.

A4 Very little is usually revealed and it often degenerates into point scoring.

***examiner's* note** MPs can ask for a written answer to a question and there are over 50,000 written questions each year.

***evaluation* point** Minister's Question Time could be considered as an aspect of ministerial responsibility and a more effective opportunity than Prime Minister's Question Time for MPs to hold ministers to account.

House of Lords: key terms and concepts

Q1 What were hereditary peers?

Q2 What are life peers?

Q3 What are 'crossbenchers'?

Q4 What is the Salisbury Convention?

ANSWERS

A1 Members of the House of Lords whose right to sit and vote in the chamber was derived from a title inherited within the family.

A2 Members of the House of Lords whose title and right to sit and vote in the chamber are not hereditary and cease upon death.

A3 Independent members of the House of Lords without party affiliation, so called because of the chamber's seating arrangements.

A4 The constitutional convention that the House of Lords does not vote on the Second reading, and therefore cannot block a government bill contained in the governing party's election manifesto.

***examiner's* note** All but 92 hereditary peers lost their voting rights in the House of Lords in 1999 when the Labour government began reforming the composition of the chamber.

***evaluation* point** Since the removal of all but 92 hereditary peers, most members of the House of Lords are life peers.

 49 **ANSWERS**

House of Lords: key legislation

Q1 What changes were brought about by the Parliament Act (1911)?

Q2 How did the Parliament Act (1949) change things?

Q3 Outline the main change brought about by the Life Peerages Act (1958).

Q4 What was the main change introduced by the House of Lords Act (1999)?

ANSWERS

A1 This Act was the statute that confirmed the subordinate role of the House of Lords to the House of Commons. The Lords could no longer reject legislation outright, but merely delay it.

A2 It reduced the delaying power of the House of Lords further.

A3 It introduced life peerages for both men and women whose title and rights to sit and vote in the chamber are not hereditary but cease upon death.

A4 All but 92 hereditary peers lost their right to vote and sit in the House of Lords.

***examiner's* note** In 1963 any heir to a hereditary peerage was allowed to renounce their title (e.g. Tony Benn).

***evaluation* point** Labour in 1997 appeared to have a clearer idea of what they disliked (hereditary peers) than about what positive measures should be taken to reform the Lords overall.

 **ANSWERS**

Lords reform 1997–2010

Q1 How did New Labour reform the House of Lords?

Q2 Why was there not further reform of the Lords?

Q3 Was New Labour's reform of the Lords a success or a failure?

ANSWERS

A1 It removed all but 92 of the hereditary peers from sitting and voting in the Lords.

A2 No consensus could be reached particularly on the composition of the Lords, whether it should be wholly or partially elected.

A3 Success. The removal of all but 92 hereditaries was a major reform. The House of Lords became more effective.

Failure. It failed to achieve the next stage of reform: a wholly or partially elected House.

examiner's note The Conservative–Lib Dem coalition government is committed to moving towards a wholly or mainly elected Lords.

evaluation point A move to wholly or mainly elected Lords would raise questions about whether its powers should be increased.

Should the Lords be wholly elected?

Q1 What are the main arguments for a wholly elected Lords?

Q2 What are the arguments against a wholly elected Lords?

Q3 Which side of the argument do you support, and why?

ANSWERS ❯❯

A1 A fully elected Lords whould have the legitimacy conferred by democratic elections. More representative of the electorate, particularly if elected by PR. Scrutiny function enhanced by having been elected.

A2 Possible conflict with Commons, both claiming democratic legitimacy. Could produce gridlock. An appointed House has expertise and independence. More party control by the whips.

A3 Decide which arguments you find most persuasive, state them and refute those on the other side.

***examiner's* note** In a modern democracy it is difficult to support one of the two houses of the legislature not being elected.

***evaluation* point** There are 66 countries with second chambers, of which 48 are either directly or indirectly elected.

Local government

Q1 What does local government consist of?

Q2 Define the terms 'ward' and 'councillor'.

Q3 By what means does central government control local government?

Q4 What is meant by the term *ultra vires* with regard to local authorities?

ANSWERS

A1 Local government varies significantly. Most areas still operate under a two-tier system (borough/district council and county council), but some have become unitary authorities.

A2 A ward is an electoral district within a local council area. A councillor is an individual elected to represent a ward.

A3 Through statute (under *ultra vires*); through inspections and acting in default (where a council fails to discharge its duties properly); through adjusting its grant to local authorities and/or capping the level of local government taxation.

A4 They can only do what is authorised by law. Anything else is *ultra vires* (beyond their authority). Councillors can be prosecuted and fined.

examiner's note In the 1980s, the Conservative government threatened default proceedings against Norwich City Council over its failure to implement 'Right to Buy' legislation.

evaluation point Some see low turnout in local elections as a consequence of low regard for local government.

Regional government

Q1 What is the 'West Lothian Question'?

Q2 Identify the main units of regional government that exist in the UK.

Q3 How and when were these institutions established?

ANSWERS

A1 Posed by West Lothian MP Tam Dalyell in the 1970s: what should be done about devolution giving Scottish MSPs control of most areas of policy in Scotland, while MPs representing Scottish constituencies at Westminster (e.g. Dalyell) could still vote on bills determining policy for England?

A2 Scottish Parliament, Welsh Assembly, Northern Ireland Assembly and their respective executives.

A3 The Scottish Parliament and Welsh Assembly were established by Act of Parliament and approved by referendums in September 1997; first elections in 1999. The Northern Ireland Assembly was the product of the Good Friday Agreement, confirmed by referendum in May 1998; first elections in June 1998.

examiner's note Further reducing the number of Scottish MPs at Westminster would help to address the West Lothian Question.

evaluation point The Northern Ireland referendum on the Good Friday Agreement produced an 81% turnout and a 71% 'yes' vote.

Devolved assemblies

Q1 How does the scope and extent of the Scottish Parliament's power differ from that of the Welsh Assembly?

Q2 Outline one reason why the devolution of power to Scotland, Wales and Northern Ireland has led to calls for the establishment of English regional assemblies.

Q3 Identify one or more ways in which devolution has brought different government policies to the people of Scotland.

ANSWERS

A1 The Scottish Parliament exercises primary legislative authority over most policy areas in Scotland and has tax-varying powers. The Welsh Assembly has secondary legislative powers, cannot make or amend laws alone, or vary taxes; it simply consults and makes policy proposals.

A2 Those living in Scotland, Wales and Northern Ireland are represented in the Westminster Parliament as well as in their devolved institutions, so it has been argued that English voters are under-represented.

A3 The Labour–Lib Dem coalition in Scotland (1999–2007) adopted different policies on student finance and nursing care for the elderly.

***examiner's* note** The minority Labour administration resulting from the first Welsh Assembly elections in 1999 eventually became a Lib–Lab coalition. After the 2003 elections, the assembly returned to one-party control under Labour. After elections in 2007 Labour entered into a coalition with Plaid Cymru.

***evaluation* point** In 1999, the SNP argued that devolution would make it inappropriate for Scottish MPs at Westminster to vote on laws that did not affect their own constituents.

 **ANSWERS**

Development of the European Union

Q1 In 1957, the Treaty of Rome set up the European Economic Community (EEC) with six original members. True or false?

Q2 List the original members of the EEC.

Q3 Why did the UK not join the EEC in 1957?

Q4 When did the UK become a member of the EEC?

ANSWERS

A1 True.

A2 France; Germany; Italy; Belgium; the Netherlands; Luxembourg.

A3 The UK believed that its future lay with the Commonwealth and its 'special relationship' with the USA.

A4 The UK joined the EEC — later to become the European Union (EU) — in 1973.

***examiner's* note** The UK made two unsuccessful attempts to join the EEC in 1961 and 1967. Its application was vetoed by France on both occasions.

***evaluation* point** The UK joined the European Union just as the pace of its development was slowing down. Many in the UK therefore felt that membership did not bring the benefits they had been led to expect.

Institutions of the European Union (1)

Q1 List the main institutions of the EU.

Q2 What is intergovernmentalism?

Q3 What is supranationalism?

Q4 What is integration?

ANSWERS

A1 European Commission; Council of Ministers; European Council; European Parliament; European Court of Justice.

A2 Cooperation between governments of European Union member states without abandoning their national interests.

A3 Cooperation between governments and their appointees at a level that ignores national interests and considerations.

A4 The gradual unification of European Union member states through closer cooperation on economic and other policies and the strengthening of the EU's political institutions.

***examiner's* note** The EU has both intergovernmental bodies (the Council of Ministers and the European Council) and supranational bodies (the European Commission, the European Parliament and the European Court of Justice).

***evaluation* point** Integration has been a cause of conflict in the UK, with Eurosceptics opposed to further European integration.

 **ANSWERS**

Institutions of the European Union (2)

Q1 What is the European Commission?

Q2 Outline two of its functions.

Q3 What is the Council of Ministers?

Q4 Outline two of its functions.

ANSWERS

A1 The executive body of the European Union, comprising political appointees of the governments of the member states, with primary responsibility for initiating legislation.

A2 It executes and administers EU legislation and programmes. It acts as a 'guardian of the treaties', ensuring that EU law is properly applied.

A3 The most important decision-making body of the EU, comprising representatives of the government of member states and carrying out executive and legislative functions.

A4 It is the EU's legislative body. It coordinates the broad economic policies of member states.

***examiner's* note** The Council of Ministers shares legislative power with the European Parliament, with legislative proposals being initiated by the European Commission.

***evaluation* point** Commissioners do not represent the governments of their member states and are expected to adopt a supranational attitude.

Institutions of the European Union (3)

Q1 What is the European Council?

Q2 What is the only directly elected institution of the European Union?

Q3 Outline two powers of the European Parliament.

Q4 What is the role of the European Court of Justice?

ANSWERS

A1 The EU body comprising member states' heads of government (and, in the case of some members, heads of state), foreign ministers of member states and the president of the European Commission and vice-presidents.

A2 The European Parliament.

A3 It shares legislative power with the Council of Ministers. It shares budgetary authority with the Council of Ministers and can influence EU spending. It can approve/remove the European Commission.

A4 The highest court of the EU, ensuring the uniform interpretation and application of EU law and adjudicating disputes between member states.

***examiner's* note** The European Court of Justice has been described as the supreme court of the EU and should not be confused with the European Court of Human Rights.

***evaluation* point** The European Council is a political rather than a legislative body. It discusses key issues and sets the agenda and political direction for the EU.

 ANSWERS

The Single European Act

Q1 What was the centrepiece of the Single European Act achieved by the end of 1992?

Q2 What was involved in creating a single market?

Q3 Explain qualified majority voting (QMV).

Q4 How did the Single European Act strengthen the European Parliament?

ANSWERS

A1 The creation of a single European market.

A2 The removal of taxes, restrictions and regulations on the movement of goods, services, finance and people between member states.

A3 QMV is a weighted voting system, giving each member state a weighting according to its population. When introduced, it meant there had to be a combination of at least three member states for a measure to passed.

A4 There was a marginal increase in the European Parliament's influence. It had to approve proposals from the Commission and the Council of Ministers. It could also force decision-makers to renegotiate proposals, but not stop them.

***examiner's* note** Before the Single European Act, passage of most measures required unanimity; since then there has been an extension of QMV to more policy areas.

***evaluation* point** At the time, Margaret Thatcher saw this act as an extension of free market economics, whereas Jacques Delors saw it as promoting European integration.

The Maastricht Treaty

Q1 Outline the main provisions of the Maastricht Treaty.

Q2 The treaty also established the principle of subsidiarity. What does this mean?

Q3 Outline two other changes made at Maastricht.

Q4 What two exemptions were negotiated by the UK?

ANSWERS

A1 It established a blueprint for economic and monetary union (EMU), with a single currency to be established by 1999.

A2 The principle that in the European Union decisions should be taken at the lowest level of government (local, regional, national or international) compatible with efficiency and practicality.

A3 The creation of the European Union; an extension of qualified majority voting.

A4 An opt-out from stage 3 of EMU, meaning that the UK did not have to join the single currency; an opt-out from the Social Chapter.

***examiner's* note** The UK and Italy left the exchange rate mechanism in 1992 and this raised doubts at the time about the viability of EMU.

***evaluation* point** Danish voters rejected the treaty in a referendum in 1992 and there appeared to be limited support for further integration.

The Amsterdam, Nice and Lisbon Treaties

Q1 Identify two major changes brought about by the Amsterdam Treaty (1997).

Q2 Why was the Treaty of Nice (2001) needed and what did it propose?

Q3 Why was the Lisbon Treaty (2007) introduced?

ANSWERS

A1 The treaty extended the co-decision procedure — the right of the European Parliament to amend EU legislation — into most areas of policy. It confirmed the incorporation of the Social Chapter into EU treaties.

A2 EU enlargement and the changes in EU organisation that would follow it. It proposed the restructuring of the European Commission (one commissioner for each member state); the reworking of the Council of Ministers' system of qualified majority voting (QMV) in light of enlargement.

A3 The Lisbon Treaty sought to bring into effect many of the measures originally included in the abandoned draft EU constitution.

***examiner's* note** In 2009 the UK, Germany, France and Italy each had 29 votes (out of 345) under the reformed QMV system; 255 votes were needed to pass a measure, along with the support of states representing in excess of 311 million citizens.

***evaluation* point** The extension of QMV and the reallocation of votes make it more difficult for a small number of countries to block policy.

A new constitution for the European Union

Q1 Why was a new EU constitution considered necessary in 2004?

Q2 Outline the main elements of the constitution agreed in June 2004.

Q3 Outline one argument for and one argument against the proposed EU constitution.

ANSWERS

A1 To draw together and codify the treaties and agreements constituting the EU, following more than a decade of reform that culminated in the enlargement of the EU from 15 to 25 members in May 2004.

A2 It set out the extent of EU power, restructured the EU following enlargement (e.g. reworking of QMV) and redefined the role and power of EU institutions.

A3 Supporters saw the constitution as an effective barrier to the extension of EU power. Critics saw it as a step towards a 'United States of Europe'.

examiner's note Although the constitution was abandoned, much of what it proposed was ultimately included in the Lisbon Treaty (2007).

evaluation point UK voters were not offered a referendum on the Lisbon Treaty because it was argued that it was not as far-reaching as the constitution it replaced.

 63 ANSWERS

Is there a democratic deficit in the EU?

Q1 Present the case for a democratic deficit.

Q2 Present the case against a democratic deficit.

Q3 Which side of the argument do you support, and why?

ANSWERS

A1 Legislation is initiated by the Commission which is not directly elected. Directly elected European Parliament has too few powers. Turnout is low, and European Parliament elections are often dominated by national issues. Qualified majority voting means national governments may be out-voted.

A2 The Commission is accountable to the European Parliament. National governments are represented in the Council of Ministers and the European Council. The Parliament shares legislative power in most policy areas with the Council. EU does not have power in key areas of national life, e.g. taxation.

A3 Decide which arguments you find most persuasive, state them and refute those on the other side.

examiner's note Direct election of the president of the Commission and strengthening the Parliament are proposed as ways of dealing with the democratic deficit.

evaluation point It could be argued that the model of the democratic nation state should not be used to criticise arrangments at the European level.

The prime minister: key terms

Q1 What is cabinet government?

Q2 Explain 'first among equals' *(primus inter pares)* in relation to the prime minister.

Q3 What is prime-ministerial government?

Q4 Define core executive theory.

ANSWERS

A1 The theory on the location of power in government that states that decision-making in the executive rests with the cabinet, chaired by the prime minister.

A2 The prime minister chairs the cabinet and works with other cabinet ministers to reach decisions in a system of cabinet government.

A3 The theory that the prime minister has achieved a dominant and almost presidential position, to the detriment of traditional cabinet government.

A4 Executive decisions are taken by a network of institutions operating at the heart of government, with the prime minister in a central position.

***examiner's* note** Neither 'cabinet government' nor 'prime-ministerial government' is an adequate description of where power lies or how it is exercised in the executive.

***evaluation* point** Core executive theory is an attempt to advance the debate on power in the executive beyond the focus on prime-ministerial government versus cabinet government.

ANSWERS

Role and powers of the prime minister

Q1 State four key powers of the prime minister.

Q2 Suggest two constraints on the prime minister's powers of patronage.

Q3 Are there limits to the prime minister's management of the agenda of cabinet meetings? Explain your answer.

Q4 What key power has the prime minister now relinquished?

ANSWERS

A1 The prime minister: appoints and dismisses ministers; appoints and dismisses cabinet committees; chairs the cabinet; reshuffles the cabinet.

A2 The cabinet needs to be 'balanced' (e.g. by gender, geographically, ideologically). Cabinet members must also be of a suitable calibre.

A3 A senior minister or a group of ministers may insist on a specific item being discussed. Certain items appear as a formality.

A4 The power to determine the date of the next general election.

***examiner's* note** The Conservative–Lib Dem coalition government has decided on fixed terms for parliament.

***evaluation* point** Is the prime minister of a coalition government going to be a less powerful prime minister? Look for evidence.

A prime minister's department?

Q1 What is the role of the Prime Minister's Office?

Q2 List four main units of the Prime Minister's Office.

Q3 Why was the Prime Minister's Office reorganised in 2001?

Q4 Is there now a prime minister's department?

ANSWERS 〉〉

A1 To provide support and advice across the range of prime ministerial responsibilities.

A2 Private Office; Press Office; Policy Unit; Political Office.

A3 To strengthen the Prime Minister's Office in directing and coordinating government activity more effectively.

A4 Not in a formal sense, but the changes to the Prime Minister's Office since 2001 have created a prime minister's department in all but name.

examiner's **note** Even with a reorganised Prime Minister's Office, the prime minister still does not have a great deal of support compared to a minister in charge of a Whitehall department.

evaluation **point** The case for the prime minister being able to have information and expertise comparable to cabinet colleagues needs to be balanced with the democratic desire to avoid enhancing further the powers of the prime minister.

Blair and Brown as prime ministers

Q1 How powerful a prime minister was Tony Blair?

Q2 How was Blair able to be so powerful?

Q3 What kind of prime minister was Gordon Brown?

ANSWERS ▶▶

A1 Words such as 'Napoleonic', a 'command premiership' and the 'presidentialisation' of the office of prime minister have been used to describe his premiership. Preferred 'sofa government' to cabinet government. Strengthened the Prime Minister's Office.

A2 Big parliamentary majorities in 1997 and 2001. Strong position within the party. Largely loyal cabinet.

A3 A good start but soon lost authority. Dithering over whether to call an election in 2007 was a turning-point. Seen as indecisive. Credit crunch, the recession and Purnell's cabinet resignation in 2009 added to his trouble. A failed and flawed PM?

***examiner's* note** Blair not a lame duck after 2005. Extended public sector reform agenda and brokered return of devolution in Northern Ireland.

***evaluation* point** Blair's power was restrained by 'dual monarchy', i.e. the different spheres of influence and power of Blair and Brown.

The cabinet

Q1 What is the cabinet?

Q2 Why must cabinet ministers be Members of Parliament?

Q3 Outline the key functions of the cabinet.

Q4 Define cabinet government.

ANSWERS

A1 The government committee chaired by the prime minister, comprising the leading ministers in charge of departments of state.

A2 Because the UK has a parliamentary system whereby ministers are accountable to Parliament for their actions.

A3 Registering decisions made in cabinet committees; handling political crises; discussing major issues; receiving reports on recent developments; settling disputes between departments.

A4 The theory on the location of power in government that states that decision making in the executive rests with the cabinet, chaired by the prime minister.

***examiner's* note** Most cabinet ministers are in the Commons, so they are accountable to the democratically elected chamber.

***evaluation* point** The growing infrequency of cabinet meetings under Blair was strong evidence for the absence of cabinet government but more frequent cabinet meetings and consultation with colleagues might be neccessary to make the coalition government work.

 ANSWERS

The Cabinet Office

Q1 How did Labour change the structure of the Cabinet Office after 1998?

Q2 What does the modern Cabinet Office consist of?

Q3 To what extent has the reorganisation of the Cabinet Office led to a strengthening of prime-ministerial power?

ANSWERS

A1 Labour combined several new bodies with other previously independent ones, in a Cabinet Office that many saw as a prime minister's department in all but name.

A2 Consisting of around 2,000 staff, from 1998 it included a Cabinet Office minister (the 'cabinet enforcer'), a cabinet secretary, four separate secretariats, a Performance and Innovation Unit, a Women's Unit, a Centre for Management and Policy Studies, a head of the Government and Communication Service and a chief scientific adviser.

A3 The *Guardian* and others argued that the physical centralisation of the Cabinet Office — with staff from 17 former Cabinet Office buildings relocating to Downing Street — enhanced prime-ministerial control over the cabinet.

examiner's note The Cabinet Office is a key element in the core executive.

evaluation point Despite Labour's changes, the prime minister's resources are still less than those of a minister managing a major department.

Cabinet committees

Q1 What is a cabinet committee?

Q2 Distinguish between standing and ad hoc cabinet committees.

Q3 Why are cabinet committees important?

Q4 Why have they been criticised?

ANSWERS

A1 A group of cabinet ministers selected by the prime minister to discuss and decide on a particular issue or policy area before reporting to the full cabinet.

A2 Standing committees are permanent, but ad hoc committees are temporary.

A3 They are where key issues are resolved and policies decided.

A4 For taking power away from the full cabinet (the decline of cabinet government) and increasing the power of the prime minister.

***examiner's* note** Little was known about cabinet committees until John Major published details of their structure and membership in 1992.

***evaluation* point** Cabinet committees can be seen as an extension of the cabinet system, reflecting the complexity of modern government, rather than as evidence for the decline of cabinet government.

Collective responsibility

Q1 Define collective cabinet responsibility.

Q2 Give examples of two resignations based on this convention.

Q3 Why are there so few such resignations?

Q4 Give an example of a failure to resign.

ANSWERS ▸▸

A1 A convention whereby members of the cabinet are jointly responsible for its decisions. Failure to abide by collective responsibility can result in resignation or dismissal from the government.

A2 Robin Cook in 2003 because he opposed the invasion of Iraq. James Purnell in 2009 because he could no longer support Brown as prime minister.

A3 Many MPs see themselves as career politicians and do not wish to relinquish office, having worked hard to reach the top.

A4 Eurosceptics such as Michael Portillo did little to hide their disagreement with John Major over his policy on Europe, yet remained in his government.

examiner's note Do not confuse collective responsibility with individual ministerial responsibility.

evaluation point The nature of collective responsibility is changing. Originally it applied only to the cabinet, but now it appears to have been extended to all members of the government.

Ministers and ministerial responsibility

Q1 How many ministers are there in the UK government?

Q2 Outline four key roles performed by ministers.

Q3 What is individual ministerial responsibility?

Q4 Give two examples of resignations due to individual ministerial responsibility.

ANSWERS ▶▶

A1 Over 100, including cabinet ministers, ministers of state and parliamentary undersecretaries.

A2 Policy leadership; representing departmental interests; departmental management; relations with Parliament.

A3 Ministers are answerable to Parliament for their own conduct (personal responsibility), the performance of their department and the actions and omissions of subordinates in the department (role responsibility).

A4 David Blunkett in 2005 because he broke the Ministerial Code on private sector jobs. Peter Hain in 2008 when police were investigating political donations.

examiner's **note** Norman Lamont did not resign as chancellor of the exchequer when sterling left the exchange rate mechanism in 1992.

evaluation **point** The creation of executive agencies has implications for individual ministerial responsibility. In 1995 Home Secretary Michael Howard dismissed Derek Lewis, chief executive of the prison service, holding him responsible for prison escapes.

The civil service

Q1 By whom are government departments staffed?

Q2 List the three principles traditionally applied to the civil service.

Q3 What do these three principles tell us about how the civil service should operate?

Q4 How have these principles come under strain in recent years?

ANSWERS

A1 Unelected and politically neutral civil servants appointed by the Crown.

A2 Impartiality; anonymity; permanence.

A3 Civil servants serve the Crown, not the government or a political party. Individual civil servants should not be identified publicly as the source of policy advice. They remain in post when there is a change of government.

A4 Civil servants have leaked information, raising questions about their impartiality. The increased use of special advisers has also caused problems.

***examiner's* note** The civil service is often simply referred to as 'Whitehall', due to the location of its most important offices in central London.

***evaluation* point** In 2001–02, disputes within the Department of Transport, Local Government and the Regions between the minister Stephen Byers, his media adviser Jo Moore and civil servant Martin Sixsmith ultimately cost all three their jobs.

The role of the civil service

Q1 List four functions of the civil service within the core executive.

Q2 Outline two concerns about how civil servants have performed these functions.

Q3 What reforms did the Fulton Report (1968) recommend?

Q4 How did Margaret Thatcher view the civil service?

ANSWERS

A1 Policy advice; policy consultation; policy implementation; departmental administration.

A2 In the 1970s and 1980s there were concerns that civil servants had too much influence on the policy process. The Ministry of Agriculture, Fisheries and Food was seen for many years as too sympathetic to farmers at the expense of consumers.

A3 Changes to recruitment and training; a new Civil Service Department to manage the civil service. However, little seemed to change.

A4 She viewed the civil service as inefficient, badly managed and unresponsive.

***examiner's* note** Margaret Thatcher and John Major introduced reforms that transformed the civil service, e.g. the introduction of Next Steps agencies such as the Prisons Service, contracting out services to the private sector and the Private Finance Initiative.

***evaluation* point** The size of the civil service fell from 732,000 in 1979 to 500,000 when the Conservatives left office in 1997.

 **75 ANSWERS**

Civil service reform, 1979–97

Q1 What changes were brought about by the Financial Management Initiative (1982) and Lord Rayner's Efficiency Unit?

Q2 How did the 1988 'Next Steps' report change the civil service?

Q3 What was 'market-testing'?

Q4 How did the Citizen's Charter aim to change the provision of public services?

ANSWERS

A1 Great efficiency improvements achieved by cutting costs and job losses.

A2 By the creation of semi-autonomous Next Steps agencies separating policy implementation from policy making. Implementation and the delivery of public services were transferred from existing departments to new executive agencies.

A3 The policy that activities provided by public bodies such as government departments should be subject to tests for efficiency, including outside bids to provide services.

A4 By promoting quality, choice, standards and value in the provision of public services, e.g. setting and monitoring performance targets in the NHS.

***examiner's* note** The Passport Agency, the Prison Service and the Child Support Agency are examples of Next Steps agencies.

***evaluation* point** The Private Finance Initiative was set up in 1992 to involve the private sector in public sector capital spending projects and by 1995 over £2 billion of activities had been market-tested.

The civil service under New Labour

Q1 Did Labour extend or stop the process of creating executive agencies that had begun under Margaret Thatcher with the Next Steps programme?

Q2 What was meant by the term 'joined-up government'?

Q3 What happened to John Major's Citizen's Charter once he had left office?

Q4 Did the civil service become more, or less, politicised under New Labour?

ANSWERS

A1 Extend.

A2 The idea that there should be more effective coordination between government departments, with individual departments looking to the 'bigger picture' rather than becoming too parochial.

A3 Major's Citizen's Charter effectively re-emerged as Labour's 'Service First' programme in 1998.

A4 The rise of special advisers in Labour's first term led to accusations of politicisation. The Committee on Standards in Public Life (2003) suggested classifying special advisers differently from civil servants. The Phillis Report (2004) sought to reassert civil service neutrality requirements.

examiner's note The civil service now consists of around 500,000 individuals employed in 24 government departments and over 60 agencies.

evaluation point Though Labour ridiculed the Citizen's Charter while in opposition, once in power it did create a culture of service within the public sector.

 **77** ANSWERS

Quangos

Q1 What are quangos?

Q2 Identify four broad types of quango.

Q3 Identify two arguments for and two arguments against the use of quangos.

ANSWERS

A1 Quasi-autonomous non-governmental organisations: quasi (semi) autonomous (independent) because they work with a degree of independence; non-governmental because their members are not normally chosen from elected politicians or the civil service.

A2 advisory; regulatory; administrative; spending.

A3 *Positive*: In certain areas, e.g. regulation, a degree of independence is particularly helpful. By focusing on one area, quangos often avoid problems caused by conflicting priorities in government. *Negative*: Quangos are not accountable to voters for their decisions, so there is a democratic deficit. Their meetings are often secretive and their recommendations are often not made fully public.

examiner's note The Conservative–Lib Dem coalition government has promised to reduce the number of quangos. How successful have they been?

evaluation point Quango membership can be controversial. Professor Richard Lacey's omission from SEAC (the body looking into BSE) was widely seen as politically motivated, as he had been critical of government policy.

Special advisers

Q1 What are special advisers and how did their numbers grow in the wake of Labour's 1997 general election victory?

Q2 Identify the main roles of a special adviser.

Q3 Suggest one reason why Labour made so much use of such individuals.

Q4 Identify the way in which the rise of special advisers can be seen to undermine traditional civil service principles.

ANSWERS

A1 Technically, civil servants. There were 36 special advisers in the last year of John Major's government and 69 by the end of the first year of the new Labour government in 1997.

A2 To reduce government reliance on the civil service; to help the prime minister keep up with government departments that are often far better staffed and resourced than himself.

A3 Some argue it stemmed from Labour's mistrust of the higher echelons of the civil service, particularly following the perceived politicisation of the civil service under the Conservatives.

A4 Special advisers do not appear to uphold 'impartiality' or 'anonymity', and are unlikely to survive a change in government (undermining 'permanence').

examiner's note Each cabinet minister can appoint two special advisers. Some lower-ranking ministers may also appoint them.

evaluation point Some argue that we are moving to a US-style system where the upper echelons of the bureaucracy are politicised.

 79 ANSWERS

Functions of parties

Q1 What is a political party?

Q2 List the key functions of political parties.

Q3 Distinguish between a political party and a pressure group.

Q4 How do parties promote democracy?

ANSWERS

A1 An organisation whose members share a common ideology and views on policy. Parties aim to participate in government by winning general elections and forming a government.

A2 Representation; recruitment of leaders; policy formulation; participation and mobilisation; providing stable government.

A3 Political parties run for election and, on winning, implement a range of policies. Pressure groups rarely put themselves up for election and tend to be single-issue groups or groups representing sectional interests.

A4 By offering voters a choice in terms of policies and ideology at elections; by providing voters with an opportunity to participate in the political process; by representing different classes and viewpoints.

***examiner's* note** Environmental pressure groups have succeeded in ensuring that all main parties now have environmental policies.

***evaluation* point** The Green Party began as virtually a single-issue pressure group, but it has had to develop a range of policies to improve its electoral prospects and won its first seat at Westminster in the 2010 general election.

 80 **ANSWERS**

A two-party system?

Q1 What is a two-party system?

Q2 Present two advantages of a two-party system.

Q3 Present two disadvantages of a two-party system.

Q4 Does the UK have a two-party system?

A1 A political system in which only two parties compete for office in elections with a realistic chance of forming a government.

A2 One party normally wins a clear majority, leading to strong government. The elected government is accountable because an alternative government is waiting, often highlighting the government's mistakes.

A3 It can lead to adversarial, 'see-saw' politics. The parties may be less effective at representing their members' interests, as they are forced to become overly broad churches.

A4 Yes, because Labour and the Conservatives still have most seats in the Commons. No, because after the 2010 general election there was a coalition government including the Liberal Democrats, not one of the so-called two big parties.

***examiner's* note** There is a possibility that as a result of the 2010 general election the UK may move into a different party system.

***evaluation* point** Reforms introduced by the Conservative–Lib Dem coalition may change the party system.

 ANSWERS

Adversarial and consensus politics

Q1 What is adversarial politics?

Q2 What is consensus politics?

Q3 When did the UK have a period of consensus politics?

Q4 Why did consensus politics break down?

ANSWERS

A1 Antagonistic competition between two main political parties offering to implement contrasting policies and programmes in government.

A2 Broad agreement between the main parties on a range of issues, resulting in continuity of policy following a change of government.

A3 From 1945 to 1979 there was a consensus between the Conservative and Labour parties which was at its strongest in the 1950s.

A4 Pressures caused by socioeconomic changes, especially the decline in manufacturing and the onset of recession.

***examiner's* note** Margaret Thatcher's victory for the Conservative Party in 1979 and her New Right agenda represented a decisive break with the post-1945 consensus.

***evaluation* point** The post-1945 consensus was a left-of-centre consensus whereas the post-1979 consensus is a right-of-centre consensus.

 ANSWERS

Multi-party systems

Q1 What is a multi-party system?

Q2 List two advantages of multi-party systems.

Q3 List two disadvantages of multi-party systems.

Q4 Is the UK becoming a multi-party system?

ANSWERS

A1 A political system in which more than two parties exist and contest elections with a realistic prospect of achieving political power.

A2 Voters have a wide choice. Voters are more likely to vote for a party that reflects their views. If a coalition is necessary, the ruling parties will have to compromise to achieve power.

A3 Small parties can wield disproportionate influence in forming coalition governments. The withdrawal of small parties can cause the coalition to collapse.

A4 The share of the vote of the two main parties has declined from 90% or more in the 1950s to 65% in the 2010 general election. The Liberal Democrats were in coalition after the 2010 general election.

***examiner's* note** Multi-party systems usually operate under proportional representation systems and result in coalitions.

***evaluation* point** The absence of PR for Westminster elections means genuine multi-party politics is unlikely.

 ANSWERS

Dominant-party systems

Q1 What is a single-party system?

Q2 What is a dominant-party system?

Q3 Outline one problem associated with dominant-party systems.

Q4 Is the UK a dominant-party system?

ANSWERS

A1 A political system in which there is only one ruling party and opposition parties are banned.

A2 A political system in which many political parties may exist and contest elections but only one party tends to win and dominate government.

A3 It can result in accusations of politicisation, patronage and corruption, e.g. accusations of 'sleaze' during the period of Conservative dominance, 1979–97.

A4 No, but there have been periods of continuous rule by one party, e.g. the Conservatives won four elections in a row (1979, 1983, 1987 and 1992) and now Labour has won three in a row (1997, 2001 and 2005).

***examiner's* note** The Liberal Democratic Party in Japan held power continuously between 1955 and 1993.

***evaluation* point** Labour's period of dominance ended in 2010 with the formation of a coalition government.

Two-, three- or dominant-party system?

Q1 Argue the case that the UK has a two-party system.

Q2 Present the case that the UK has a three-party system.

Q3 Argue the case that the UK has a dominant-party system.

Q4 Which system best describes the UK at present?

A1 Between 1945 and 2010 Conservative and Labour have alternated in government, so in terms of winning elections there was a two-party system.

A2 Three parties share most of the votes cast at general elections, and after the 2010 general election the Liberal Democrats went into government with the Conservatives.

A3 The Conservatives were in power from 1979 to 1997 and Labour from 1997 to 2010.

A4 A dominant-party system best describes the UK between 1979 and 2010, with a period of Conservative dominance followed by a period of New Labour dominance.

***examiner's* note** On the basis of percentage share of the vote it is possible to argue for a three-party system.

***evaluation* point** Liberal Democrat participation in government after the 2010 general election reinforces the idea of a three-party system.

 **85** **ANSWERS**

Internal party democracy

Q1 How democratic is the process by which the main UK political parties elect their leaders?

Q2 Is the way in which the main parties select their candidates for parliamentary election best seen as 'top-down' or 'bottom-up'?

Q3 Which of the three main UK political parties formulates its policies in the most democratic way?

ANSWERS

A1 All three parties involve their members. The Liberal Democratic leader is elected under one member, one vote (OMOV). The Conservative Party does use OMOV, but only after the party's MPs have finalised a choice of two candidates. Labour also uses OMOV, but its members only constitute one-third of the Electoral College that selects the leader.

A2 Ostensibly, all choose candidates locally, but those selected must be taken from lists of centrally approved candidates. The Labour Party allows the central party to impose a candidate upon a constituency.

A3 The Liberal Democrats. Their annual national conference remains the party's sovereign policy-making body.

***examiner's* note** In 2001 the Labour Party was accused of 'parachuting' millionaire Tory defector Shaun Woodward into the safe Labour seat of St Helen's, against the wishes of the constituency party.

***evaluation* point** With party memberships falling and members tending to be more ideologically driven, candidates chosen by the party members might lack appeal to the broader electorate.

 **ANSWERS**

Party finance

Q1 Identify traditional sources of party finance for the two main parties in the UK.

Q2 In what respects has the basis of Labour Party funding changed in recent years?

Q3 Give an example of the efforts that have been made to regulate party funding.

ANSWERS

A1 Traditionally, the Labour Party was funded largely by trade unions through affiliation fees. The Conservative Party was supported by wealthy business interests.

A2 The reforms made by Neil Kinnock, John Smith and Tony Blair reduced the power of the unions in the party. At the same time, the party attracted high-profile donations from wealthy individuals, e.g. Bernie Ecclestone, Lord Sainsbury and Lord Hamlyn.

A3 The Political Parties, Elections and Referendum Act (2000) set an upper limit on national campaign expenditure by political parties at general elections (£30,000 per constituency). Nationally, parties were required to declare publicly all donations over £5,000.

***examiner's* note** Falling individual membership has forced parties to court wealthy individual backers.

***evaluation* point** In the 1990s, large individual donations led to the perception that one could 'buy influence', e.g. Bernie Ecclestone, supposedly in return for a sympathetic ear on tobacco advertising in Formula 1.

 87 ANSWERS

Party ideology

Q1 What ideological positions were traditionally associated with the Conservative Party and the Labour Party?

Q2 In what respect have these parties shifted from their traditional ideological positions?

Q3 Why do some commentators refer to an 'end of ideology'?

ANSWERS

A1 The Labour Party was formed by trade unions and socialist societies, so it has been regarded as a socialist party for most of its existence. The Conservative Party traditionally favoured pragmatism and believed in gradual improvements founded on experience and existing institutions, rather than *a priori* reasoning and radical change.

A2 Labour distanced itself from socialism under Tony Blair, e.g. redrafting Clause IV. Margaret Thatcher abandoned a traditional conservative approach by adopting a radical neo-liberal agenda. More recently, David Cameron tried to re-brand the Conservative party by focusing on environmental policy and social exclusion.

A3 The two main political parties are no longer ideologically distinct. They appear to be arguing over the tone and presentation of policy rather than its substance.

***examiner's* note** David Cameron, like his predecessor, Michael Howard, endeavoured to moderate his party's positions on homosexuality and on welfare.

***evaluation* point** Ideological convergence in mainstream politics may have led to the rise of minor parties in recent years.

 **88** ANSWERS

Minor parties

Q1 Identify some of the different kinds of minor party that operate in the UK.

Q2 Identify one reason why minor parties have traditionally found it difficult to achieve electoral success in the UK.

Q3 Give two reasons why minor parties have become more popular in recent years.

ANSWERS

A1 Regional (e.g. Plaid Cymru); single-issue (e.g. UKIP); ideological (e.g. BNP).

A2 The first-past-the-post electoral system, employed in virtually all elections before 1997, made it difficult for smaller parties as they had to win a large proportion of the vote in a constituency before they had any chance of winning.

A3 The tendency of the big parties to move towards the centre ground has forced many who would previously have supported such parties into the arms of minor parties. The adoption of proportional or hybrid electoral systems in some UK elections has also benefited such parties.

examiner's **note** The existence of groups such as UKIP, the ProLife Alliance and the Referendum Party blurs the distinction between parties and pressure groups.

evaluation **point** Minor parties are more likely to succeed electorally with low turnouts, as their support tends to be more committed.

 89 **ANSWERS**

Pressure groups and democracy

Q1 What is pluralism?

Q2 Suggest two ways in which pressure groups can be seen to enhance democracy.

Q3 Suggest two ways in which pressure groups can be seen as a threat to democracy.

Q4 Which side of the argument do you support, and why?

ANSWERS

A1 A system of government that allows and encourages public participation, particularly through the activities of competing pressure groups.

A2 They allow participation between elections. They give a voice to minority groups.

A3 Well-organised minorities can drown out the voice of the general public. Single-issue groups can channel enthusiasm away from elections.

A4 Yes, they support democracy because they allow minorities to be heard. No, they are a threat to democracy because they focus on a single issue that may not have majority support.

examiner's note The UK is often seen as a pluralist democracy with competing pressure groups and the government acting as referee.

evaluation point Pluralism is not fully achieved in the UK because of inequality of access and influence amongst competing pressure groups.

Types of pressure group

Q1 Distinguish between sectional and cause groups.

Q2 Give three examples each of sectional and cause groups.

Q3 What is a peak or 'umbrella' pressure group?

Q4 Why might some pressure groups be temporary?

ANSWERS

A1 Sectional groups represent the shared interests of a particular section of society whereas cause groups promote an interest or idea not of direct personal benefit to its members.

A2 *Sectional*: British Medical Association; Law Society; National Farmers' Union. *Cause*: Greenpeace; Amnesty International; Royal Society for the Protection of Birds.

A3 An organisation that speaks for a variety of smaller groups with similar interests, e.g. the Trades Union Congress (TUC) and the Confederation of British Industry (CBI).

A4 They might disband once they have achieved their objective, e.g. stopping the building of a new road or saving a local hospital.

examiner's note Some cause groups are permanent (e.g. Friends of the Earth) and some are temporary (e.g. Electoral Reform Society).

evaluation point The distinction between sectional and cause groups is not clear-cut. For example, teaching unions campaign for improvements in education (a 'cause'), while at the same time protecting the sectional interests of their members.

Insider and outsider pressure groups

Q1 What is an insider pressure group?

Q2 Give three examples of insider groups.

Q3 What is an outsider pressure group?

Q4 Give three examples of outsider groups.

ANSWERS

A1 A group that is particularly influential because it is regularly consulted by policy-makers such as ministers and civil servants.

A2 National Trust; Confederation of British Industry; Royal Society for the Prevention of Cruelty to Animals.

A3 A group that is not regularly consulted by policy-makers and therefore uses other methods to gain influence.

A4 Countryside Alliance; OutRage!; Keep Sunday Special.

examiner's note Some groups are outsider groups 'by necessity' because their views are not supported by key policy-makers, e.g. Campaign for Nuclear Disarmament.

evaluation point While the National Farmers' Union works in the interests of farmers, the Food Standards Agency was set up to protect the consumers.

Pressure group methods

Q1 What do we mean by the term 'traditional methods' in the context of pressure group activities?

Q2 Identify some of the less traditional methods employed by pressure groups in recent years.

Q3 Give an example of a group using legal action as a pressure group tactic.

Q4 Give examples of groups using candidacy in elections as a pressure group tactic.

ANSWERS

A1 Methods such as letter writing, circulating petitions and marches.

A2 Hauliers' use of road blockades over fuel duty; members of Fathers 4 Justice climbing Buckingham Palace dressed as Batman, and showering the prime minister with coloured flour at Question Time.

A3 The ProLife Alliance (e.g. over the application of the Human Fertilisation and Embryology Act, against abortion and in opposition to the proposed separation of conjoined twins).

A4 Referendum Party in 1997; ProLife Alliance in 1997 and 2001; Respect in the wake of the Iraq War.

***examiner's* note** The Human Rights Act (1998) has enhanced the ability of pressure groups to pursue legal remedies within the UK.

***evaluation* point** Many pressure groups are now abandoning traditional methods in favour of more innovative and/or direct tactics.

The new politics of pressure

Q1 Pressure group activity is growing. True or false?

Q2 Why is this happening?

Q3 Why are many of the new groups outsider groups?

Q4 What tactics are used by these groups?

ANSWERS ≫

A1 True. For example, the Royal Society for the Protection of Birds grew from 100,000 members in 1972 to 1,000,000 in 1997.

A2 A rise in living standards means that people have more time, freedom and money to participate in causes in which they believe.

A3 Many protesters are concerned about globalisation or the environment and have members who relish a battle with the state or transnational companies.

A4 Dramatic tactics, such as civil disobedience and non-violent direct action, are often used, e.g. by anti-road protesters, animal rights activists and anti-globalisation protesters.

***examiner's* note** Many groups are protesting against the results of the affluence that gives them the freedom to protest, e.g. using mobile phones to coordinate protests against the siting of mobile phone masts.

***evaluation* point** More and more inventive tactics are being used by pressure groups, e.g. training camps to learn obstructive tactics such as tunnelling and how to build tree houses.

Direct action

Q1 What do we mean by direct action?

Q2 Identify two reasons why direct action might have become more widespread in recent years.

Q3 Give three examples of high-profile direct action campaigns.

ANSWERS

A1 Direct action starts from the premise that more visible and direct protests — often involving illegal methods or violence — offer the best opportunity of success because they make politicians take notice and can broaden public support.

A2 Disillusionment with traditional methods; a belief that direct action works (e.g. the freezing of the 'fuel escalator' in the wake of the fuel protests in 2000).

A3 Hunt saboteurs; fuel protests; Fathers 4 Justice.

examiner's note The high-profile campaign by Fathers 4 Justice led to the Conservatives adopting many of its immediate demands.

evaluation point Direct action can be seen as undermining the principle of representative democracy. For example, by boarding Shell's Brent Spar platform in 1995, Greenpeace was able to scupper plans for deep-sea disposal. These plans were the product of many years of research and had the support of John Major's government.

Appointment of the judiciary

Q1 How were senior judges traditionally appointed?

Q2 Outline the reforms to the appointments process introduced by Labour between 1997 and 2010.

Q3 Argue in favour of an independent judicial appointments commission.

ANSWERS

A1 Traditionally, by the monarch on the advice of the prime minister and the Lord Chancellor.

A2 Under the Constitutional Reform Act (2005) an independent Judicial Appointments Commission (JAC) was established to deal with most senior appointments. Supreme Court appointments are made by the Lord Chancellor on the recommendation of a separate adhoc appointments commission.

A3 The traditional role of the Lord Chancellor and prime minister in the appointment of judges led to accusations of politicisation. Establishing such a commission served to underline the independence of the judiciary. It may also ultimately result in a senior judiciary that is more socially representative of the broader population.

***examiner's* note** Labour's reform agenda faced opposition both in the House of Lords and among senior members of the judiciary.

***evaluation* point** Judicial independence (freedom from control) is not the same as judicial impartiality (absence of bias), although the latter is often enhanced by the former.

Power of the judiciary

Q1 What do we mean by judicial review in the UK context?

Q2 How has membership of the European Community (more recently the European Union) enhanced the power of the UK judiciary?

Q3 Has the passing of the Human Rights Act (HRA) in 1998 significantly extended the power of UK courts?

ANSWERS

A1 UK courts cannot declare statutes unconstitutional as statute law is the supreme source of constitutional law. However, they can review the action of government officials and decide whether they have acted beyond the authority given to them under the law (*ultra vires*).

A2 In the *Factortame* case (1990), the European Court of Justice (ECJ) ruled that UK courts can suspend UK statutes where they appear to violate EU law, at least until the ECJ makes a final determination.

A3 Courts can now issue a declaration of incompatibility where a parliamentary statute appears to violate the rights set out in the HRA. Parliament is not, however, obliged to amend the offending statute.

***examiner's* note** The courts famously ruled that some sections of the Anti-Terrorism, Crime and Security Act (2001) were incompatible with the Human Rights Act.

***evaluation* point** Government and parliament do not have to back down. For example, the Labour government did not abandon its use of control orders.

 ANSWERS

Rights

Q1 What are 'natural rights'?

Q2 Give examples of those rights that are normally protected in liberal democracies.

Q3 Distinguish between 'positive rights' and 'negative rights'.

ANSWERS

A1 Those universal, 'God-given' and inalienable rights identified by philosophers such as John Locke, including life, liberty and property.

A2 Freedom of conscience; freedom of expression; freedom of association; freedom to protest; freedom of movement; freedom from arbitrary arrest; the right to a fair trial; freedom from torture; the right to own property.

A3 The term 'positive rights' refers to those rights explicitly assigned to citizens. 'Negative rights' are those that are not explicitly set out, but which exist in the absence of any law forbidding individuals from exercising them.

***examiner's* note** Various statutes enacted by Parliament, e.g. the Regulation of Investigatory Powers Act (2002), could be said to limit many of the freedoms outlined in A2.

***evaluation* point** The UK system has traditionally been characterised as having a system of 'negative rights', although measures such as the Human Rights Act have changed this, to a degree at least.

Redress of grievances

Q1 What is a tribunal?

Q2 Give an example of a public inquiry.

Q3 What was the Citizen's Charter?

Q4 Define the term 'ombudsman'.

ANSWERS

A1 A form of arbitration often used where there is no real remedy through the courts, either because the complainant does not have the ability (or money) to pursue the case legally or because they have been denied a judicial review.

A2 The Chilcot Inquiry into the Iraq war, which started in 2009, sought to identify those lessons that needed to be learnt from the decision to go to war.

A3 Launched in 1991, the Citizen's Charter was John Major's 'big idea'. It set out the levels of service citizens could expect from public bodies.

A4 An ombudsman investigates complaints made by the public and suggests possible redress where they find maladministration.

***examiner's* note** John Major's Citizen's Charter evolved into Labour's 'Service First' programme after 1998.

***evaluation* point** Many feel that public inquiries of the type held over Heathrow Terminal 5 are pointless, as they cost enormous amounts of money (£80 million in the case of the Heathrow Inquiry) and have no ultimate power to deflect governments from their chosen course.

 ANSWERS

The Human Rights Act

Q1 What is the Human Rights Act (HRA)?

Q2 Can UK statute be declared unconstitutional under this act?

Q3 Give an example of the HRA being used in defence of an individual's rights.

ANSWERS

A1 The HRA was passed in 1998 and came into force in October 2000. It incorporated most of the articles of the European Convention on Human Rights (1950) into UK law.

A2 No. The courts can only make a declaration of incompatibility and invite Parliament to reconsider the offending statute.

A3 The Appeal Court ruled that, in requiring a paranoid schizophrenic killer being held in Broadmoor to prove his mental health, the Mental Health Act (1983) had reversed the burden of proof (protected by HRA, Article 6) and infringed his liberty (HRA, Article 5). The authorities should have been required to prove that he was dangerous enough to warrant continued detention.

examiner's **note** The post-9/11 anti-terrorist legislation led to the suspension (or 'derogation') of some articles of the HRA.

evaluation **point** The HRA is not equivalent to the US Bill of Rights, as it is neither entrenched nor superior to regular parliamentary statute.